All the Verdis of Venice

Normand Chaurette

translated by Linda Gaboriau

Talonbooks
2000

Talonbooks
P.O. Box 2076
Vancouver, British Columbia, Canada V6B 3S3
Tel.: (604) 444-4889; Fax: (604) 444-4119; Internet: www.talonbooks.com

Typeset in New Baskerville and printed and bound in Canada by Hignell
Book Printing.

First Printing: August 2000

Talonbooks are distributed in Canada by General Distribution Services, 325
Humber College Blvd., Toronto, Ontario, Canada M9W 7C3; Tel.:(416) 213-
1919; Fax:(416) 213-1917. Talonbooks are distributed in the U.S.A. by
General Distribution Services Inc., 4500 Witmer Industrial Estates, Niagara
Falls, New York, U.S.A. 14305-1386; Tel.:1-800-805-1083; Fax:1-800-481-6207.

Je vous écris du Caire was first published in 1996 by Lémeac Éditeur Inc.,
Montréal, Québec.

Canadian Cataloguing in Publication Data

Chaurette, Normand, 1954-
[Je vous écris du Caire. English]
All the Verdis of Venice

A play.
Translation of: Je vous écris du Caire.
ISBN 0-88922-442-0

I. Gaboriau, Linda. II. Title.
PS8555.H439J413 2000   C842'.54   C00-910754-1
PQ3919.2.C5316J413 2000

The publisher gratefully acknowledges the financial support of the Canada
Council for the Arts; the Government of Canada through the Book Publishing
Industry Development Program; and the Province of British Columbia through
the British Columbia Arts Council for our publishing activities.

For Gaëtan

Je vous écris du Caire was first produced in French by Théâtre d'Aujourd'hui in Montreal in October 1993, with the following cast:

THE PROMPTER	Jean Marchand
THE DIRECTOR	Luc Durand
GUISEPPE VERDI	René Gagnon
RINUCCIO TERZIANI	Aubert Pallascio
LA STOLZ	Linda Sorgini

Directed by Alexandre Hausvater
Assisted by Suzanne Beaudry
Lighting by Guy Simard
Costumes by Véronique Borboën
Sound Design by Jean Marchand

All the Verdis of Venice was first presented in English in a staged reading co-produced by CEAD and Playwrights Workshop Montreal as part of the special event, "Theatre of Americas in Translation," at Montreal's Festival du Théâtre des Amériques in May 1995.

Characters

THE PROMPTER

MARIANI, director of la Scala

GIUSEPPE VERDI, composer

RINUCCIO TERZIANI, opera singer

TERESA STOLZ, opera singer

The action takes place at la Scala Opera House in Milan in the 1860s.

I

A room adjoining the office of the director of la Scala Opera House in Milan. It is a kind of antechamber or waiting room. Several chairs. A piano. The room is dimly lit. On the left, two doors, one leading to the office and the other to the hallway. They are colossal. On the right, a trapdoor in the floor.

THE PROMPTER enters through the trapdoor. He is old, shortsighted, a hunchback. He lights the candles on a candelabra, then sits down at the piano. He plays several notes, the first measures of an opera by Verdi. Suddenly: noise, the sound of voices. Three men enter: TERZIANI, GIUSEPPE VERDI and THE DIRECTOR. THE PROMPTER hides in a corner, observes the three men, then disappears unnoticed.

THE DIRECTOR
> *(forcing VERDI to enter, threatening him with a revolver)* Maestro Giuseppe Verdi, you have forty-eight hours to compose the opera ordered by Minister Penco.

VERDI
(*on the floor*) Don't you think it's inhuman to
hold a musician hostage, to sequester him
and condemn him to compose an opera?

THE DIRECTOR
For the morning of the 14th.

TERZIANI
Have pity on him, Signor Mariani.

VERDI
(*to THE DIRECTOR, indicating TERZIANI*) I don't
know this man.

THE DIRECTOR
Rinuccio Terziani.

VERDI
Who is he?

THE DIRECTOR
A baritone.

VERDI
(*to TERZIANI*) Terziani?

TERZIANI
Maestro.

VERDI
I thought you were dead and buried.

THE DIRECTOR
Minister Penco is on his way.

VERDI
Penco named minister!

THE DIRECTOR
He'll be here on the morning of the 14th.

VERDI
Today is the 12th!

THE DIRECTOR
The treaty has been signed. I promised him
the opera for the 12th. It's a miracle that he's
granted me forty-eight hours grace.

VERDI
I refuse.

THE DIRECTOR
This time we cannot extend the deadline.

VERDI
I refuse.

THE DIRECTOR
You have written us a hundred times to that
effect. More diplomacy and less obstinacy on
your part would have spared us all this
trouble.

VERDI
You allowed the Party leaders to believe that
you had my consent?

TERZIANI
   (*to THE DIRECTOR*) You shouldn't have gone
   ahead with the kidnapping. What will you do
   the day after tomorrow when the maestro
   publicly denounces the conditions you
   imposed on him?

VERDI
   They are expecting me in Cairo.

THE DIRECTOR
   False. You just arrived from Cairo.

VERDI
   They've had to postpone the performances
   until the embargo is lifted and the set and
   the costumes can be shipped. But I must
   finish *Aida*. I must return to Cairo.

THE DIRECTOR
   Not until you have composed my opera.

VERDI
   "Your" opera!

THE DIRECTOR
   The treaty between Austria and Italy is more
   important than the Suez Canal.

VERDI
   Forty-eight hours to compose an opera, it's
   impossible!

THE DIRECTOR
   We asked you for it a year and a half ago.

VERDI

(*to THE DIRECTOR*) Put that gun down …

*He jumps on THE DIRECTOR. The revolver
falls to the floor, THE DIRECTOR promptly picks
it up again. Standstill.*

THE DIRECTOR

When I was appointed director, I was given a
mandate, and I'm going to fulfill that
mandate. With all the new legislation,
nothing works in this country any more. The
people were the first to support Unification.
Now that political dream has become reality,
and the nation has never been so divided.

VERDI

And I'm the one who's supposed to help you
win back the trust of the people?

THE DIRECTOR

By speaking to them about things they can
understand. By speaking to them about what
they love.

VERDI

The people—

THE DIRECTOR

Music.

VERDI

I am the people.

THE DIRECTOR
   Opera.

VERDI
   And you will never win my trust.

THE DIRECTOR
   Unification was supposed to open the door to
   the future. Not create two Italys opposed to
   each other.

VERDI
   Only cityfolk talk like that.

THE DIRECTOR
   Everything we have endeavoured to create
   will only make sense the day people like
   you—

VERDI
   People like me, countryfolk, will never
   understand your endeavours.

THE DIRECTOR
   —the day people like you decide to support
   our efforts.

VERDI
   Efforts that have a single objective: to
   assassinate democracy.

THE DIRECTOR
   How can democracy thrive in a climate where
   everything we preach is abstract? If I were the
   people, I would feel demoralized too. But not

if I were given something to satisfy me. Not if the man of the hour is Maestro Verdi who knows how to rally the crowds. If the state had taken charge of your *Traviata*, it would have been a triumph. Art is made of dreams, and dreams must be national. Instead of going to live in exile in Egypt to write an exotic opera, Guiseppe Verdi, I want you to be paid for writing a national masterpiece.

VERDI
You mean a masterpiece of propaganda.

THE DIRECTOR
Not at all. A truly European drama that tells a good story with good characters who say things everyone can understand.

VERDI
Everyone can understand *Aida*.

THE DIRECTOR
But *Aida* is Egypt. I have a better suggestion: love. A story about the reconciliation of enemies.

VERDI
I refuse.

THE DIRECTOR
We've run out of pretexts to buy time. It would be disastrous if Minister Penco arrived before I can deliver my opera. That must be avoided at all costs. Here's the libretto.

VERDI
A libretto?

THE DIRECTOR
Of German inspiration, telling a Spanish
story, about Gallic heroes dealing with the
Flemish rebellion.

VERDI
What could be more Italian?

THE DIRECTOR
The music.

VERDI
(*leafing through the libretto*) Germany, Spain,
Gaul ... What is this supposed to mean?

THE DIRECTOR
It means, Maestro, that you have no time to
lose.

VERDI
People don't impose librettos on me.

THE DIRECTOR
I quite agree, most of the them are rotten.
But whose fault is that? Where are the
musicians capable of inspiring librettists?
Those provincial harmonizers? They're
burying Italy under a tradition bound to
renew nothing but its failures. We've had
enough of their insipid purring which our

adversaries quite rightly consider insignificant.

VERDI
What do you expect, with the new legislation?

THE DIRECTOR
Verdi, I want you to save us from the greatest threat to our country's glory—the presence of imperfect music. I want a total work of art. The day has come for Italy to give the world its first truly national work. I want a total opera.

VERDI
(*still leafing through the libretto*) Wait ... what is this? ... There are five acts?

THE DIRECTOR
And a prologue. Minister Penco expects a spectacular work, worthy of the Treaty between Austria and Italy.

VERDI
And the title?

THE DIRECTOR
(*to TERZIANI*) The title?

TERZIANI
(*to VERDI*) That's up to you.

THE DIRECTOR
Make it short, direct, to the point. I suggest: "Médor the Brave."

VERDI
Ha!

THE DIRECTOR
It's a perfectly fine title.

VERDI
A good name for a dog.

THE DIRECTOR
Perhaps he's not yet known as a hero, but just think, for posterity ...

TERZIANI
"Médor" ... let's see ... with a subtitle: *L'opera della reconciliazione delle due nazione* ...

THE DIRECTOR
No, a good opera should have a concise title. Let's settle for "Médor," period. It's a valiant name.

TERZIANI
"Médor" by Giuseppe Verdi.

THE DIRECTOR
Oh yes. I can already feel that title inside me. This is a historical moment. Go ahead, Verdi, begin.

VERDI
I said no.

THE DIRECTOR
What?

TERZIANI
He said no.

Pause.

VERDI
I write only for Teresa Stolz now.

THE DIRECTOR
We know that, Maestro. (*to TERZIANI*) Where
is she?

TERZIANI
(*pointing to one of the doors*) She's waiting
outside.

VERDI
What? La Stolz is here?

THE DIRECTOR
Bring her in.

TERZIANI exits.

VERDI
La Stolz? Not la Stolz!

THE DIRECTOR
Didn't you state publicly that you wanted to
hear her again? In private? Your wishes are
our desires, Maestro.

VERDI
Never. I will not be part of your scheming.

THE DIRECTOR
No one here has any choice.

TERZIANI ushers in LA STOLZ.

VERDI
Teresa Stolz!

LA STOLZ
Maestro.

VERDI
They kidnapped you, too?

LA STOLZ
On *la strada*. As I was leaving the theatre, on my way home.

THE DIRECTOR
Time is of the essence, Verdi.

VERDI
And if I refuse. (*THE DIRECTOR aims his gun at VERDI.*) Go ahead, shoot.

THE DIRECTOR aims his gun at TERZIANI.

TERZIANI
My answer is yes.

VERDI
Shoot me.

THE DIRECTOR aims his gun at LA STOLZ.

THE DIRECTOR
It would be a pity to have to find another
soprano for the lead role which, if you so
desire, Maestro, should do honour to la Stolz.

VERDI
How can you expect her to sing under such
circumstances?

LA STOLZ
If it's really Giuseppe Verdi, I'll sing.

*****

LA STOLZ
"Are you really Giuseppe Verdi?"

VERDI
"Are you really la Stolz?"

LA STOLZ
Perhaps it's la Benza imitating la Stolz?

VERDI
And the gondolier pretending to be Verdi?

LA STOLZ
The night was so uncannily bright, I felt as if
I'd stepped through a veil of light.

VERDI

I knew that la Benza could never be mistaken
for la Stolz, even wearing the most clever
disguise of the entire Carnival.

LA STOLZ

Every garland carved in the ivory of the
palazzos of Venice was framed by antique
streetlights, whose glow made all things and
all beings seem as pale as their shadows. You
were there, by the narrow canal, and I had
recognized you.

VERDI

Among a hundred look-alikes. A few feet
away, on the Ponte Rialto, they were holding
a contest.

LA STOLZ

To crown the man who looked most like you.
At first, I thought you were among the
contestants. I walked up to one of them and
said: "Tell me, please, which one is the real
Verdi?" And he answered—

VERDI

"Why, I am."

LA STOLZ

And when I turned around, there you were—

VERDI

I answered—

LA STOLZ
"I am Teresa Stolz."

They kiss. Beat.

VERDI
Wasn't anyone with you?

LA STOLZ
Of course, you must remember.

VERDI
But just now, before they forced you to come here?

LA STOLZ
Terziani was with me.

VERDI
We should leave now.

LA STOLZ
The opera director might be a clown with frightful manners, but he has fulfilled my most secret desire.

VERDI
I'm glad to hear you admit it at last, Teresa Stolz.

LA STOLZ
Do you mean you never believed in my sincerity?

VERDI

I believed you were sincere when you
referred to me as a boor and a clown, in front
of Mercadante and Benza and Colonnese. All
of Italy heard about it.

LA STOLZ

You were the first one to make comments
about me that had nothing to do with my
voice. And your comments were those of a
boor. They were rude, or rustic to say the
least.

VERDI

The village I come from is very rustic, but
very musical. Perhaps the cows' mooing
ranged from D to G sharp, but the heifers, on
the other hand—

LA STOLZ

Yes, I know, they taught you perfect pitch, you
told me all that in Venice.

VERDI

They taught me everything I know about
music.

LA STOLZ

That's not very kind to your teachers.

VERDI

They never taught me anything.

LA STOLZ

You spoke of me in vulgar terms—

VERDI

Vulgar?

LA STOLZ

A "little romp." "She and I were both drunk,
we made love all night long, tussling and
tumbling in bed, on the floor, and even at the
foot of the stairs." Our chance encounter in
Venice could only have meaning for the two
of us.

VERDI

If I was indiscreet on the subject, I must have
been drunk.

LA STOLZ

You were all too discreet afterwards, once you
were sober, in the letters you sent me. No
matter how often I reread them, not a hint of
our "romp" in Venice.

VERDI

Those letters should be burned.

LA STOLZ

They don't reflect your true thoughts?

VERDI

I wrote them knowing that other people
might read them.

LA STOLZ
Who?

VERDI
The superintendents in Cairo opened my
mail.

LA STOLZ
But I wrote to you at least twelve times. And
you wrote back.

VERDI
You have to forgive their zeal—the only
documents they ever transmitted to me were
related to state business. As for the rest, my
ordinary mail arrived in a jumble, in a box
with dozens of letters from artists I don't
know, and it's true that I probably neglected
my domestic affairs.

LA STOLZ
(*offended*) Your domestic affairs!

VERDI
So many cantatrices write to me, I don't have
time to read all the mail I receive. As a result,
I sometimes find myself face to face with
women who are total strangers, but with
whom I must pretend to pursue a
conversation I never began.

LA STOLZ
"From now on, I shall write for you and you
alone, Teresa Stolz, for it is obvious that you

seek what is true." I hope that you can at least recognize your own handwriting, Maestro.

She throws her letters at VERDI.

VERDI
"For you and you alone, Teresa Stolz ... "

LA STOLZ
Seek what is true ...

VERDI
(*as he hands the letters back to LA STOLZ*) I am the one who said that.

LA STOLZ
What an unhappy man you are!

VERDI
Yes, I am unhappy. You are Stolz's wife. And there's nothing I can do about it.

LA STOLZ
Really, Verdi! It's obvious that the *Gazetta Musicale di Milano* never reaches Cairo. You have no idea of the scandal that has tongues wagging here!

VERDI
What scandal?

LA STOLZ
Stolz and I are divorced.

VERDI

You are free!

LA STOLZ

You make those words sound as insipid as
Guelfe when he blurts them out in public.
And I haven't told you the worst news—
Guelfe has replaced Stolz at the
Conservatory.

VERDI

Guelfe has replaced Stolz?

LA STOLZ

On Penco's recommendation.

VERDI

And I am expected to write an opera for
Penco? (*He rushes to the door.*) Open the door!

LA STOLZ

Calm down.

VERDI

Let me out of here!

LA STOLZ

Stop bellowing. We can't get out of here. This
was carefully planned. They were clever
enough to intercept you at the train station.
They knew the exact time of your arrival.

VERDI

The postponement of the production in
Cairo ... the embargo ...

LA STOLZ
    We have no choice.

VERDI
    They planned it all.

LA STOLZ
    Give them *Aida*.

VERDI
    Aida? No, never.

LA STOLZ
    Well then, Giuseppe Verdi, you have
    forty-eight hours to write the opera ordered
    by Minister Penco.

                        * * * *

TERZIANI
    As we were leaving the theatre, I realized that
    we were being followed. They forced us to
    turn back, claiming there was a reception in
    honour of Mercadante. I had no reason to
    doubt them, after all, it made sense that I'd
    be invited, since I was the one who created
    the part Mercadante was singing. They had
    offered it to me again, but I was right to
    refuse.

VERDI

(*noticing the trapdoor of the prompter who has disappeared*) Look! A way out!

TERZIANI

To give this role to a baritone is to betray the composer's intentions. And for me, the composer is king. Except for Rossini, who is nothing. His works are flawed. To prove my point, some evenings, due to fatigue or whatever, one can hear nothing but the flaws. An artist can love a work unconditionally, but it can be the wrong time for him to perform it.

VERDI

That's happened to you on more than one occasion.

TERZIANI

How can you say that? You don't know me, you said so yourself.

VERDI

And I have no desire to know you.

TERZIANI

(*taking a paper out of his pocket*) *Il Corriere della sera,* February 20, 1840—"Rinuccio Terziani, a decent singer whose voice isn't that bad ... " ... And farther on ... "the minute he walks on stage, this upright citizen, despite ... " wait ... here it is: "a youthful timbre ... " (*waving the article*) "Youthful." My wife and my children

were living in a different part of Italy, and
being unable to share my glory with them
had become a familiar sacrifice.

VERDI

That article was written more than twenty
years ago.

TERZIANI

Yes, time flies. Now I have the maturity
needed for roles written for lead baritones.
Like the Ethiopian king in *Aida*. Give me that
part. You can kill two birds with one stone:
you will have your singer and Penco will have
his opera.

VERDI

Give them *Aida*? And betray the trust of the
khedive in Cairo? Neither the Party leaders,
nor you, nor anyone else will get me to
change my mind.

TERZIANI

Since they're all part of the conspiracy, we
have to accept Penco's conditions. I'll be
discreet. You can count on me. Although
public opinion will require a few white lies, I
promise to respect the official story. I swear
that when I'm released, I won't breathe a
word about the Party leaders' scheme. You
are in Cairo as we speak. Fine, but now the
director is counting on our collaboration
because the minister is a difficult man. Signor

Mariani has ordered gigantic platters of meat prepared by people he has to pay from his own pocket and who will probably have to work after the usual hours.

VERDI

That's good news, because I'm hungry.

TERZIANI

Not until you've finished your opera, I'm afraid. I know it's after midnight but as I understand it, we are expected to work on an empty stomach.

VERDI

Is that what he said?

TERZIANI

He said, "You can't write an opera on a full stomach." But he chose the right man. Just think, along with all the other honours the nation has bestowed upon you, you've been asked to produce a score for one of the ten most talented cantatrices in Italy. As for the humble baritone, yours truly—

VERDI

With his youthful timbre. Time spares no man! When I saw you, I thought I must be dealing with one of the ten most asthmatic singers in Italy.

TERZIANI

(*offended*) Why not shout it from the rooftops?

VERDI

To distinguish myself from the others who never go to hear you sing without arming themselves with tomatoes. (*He leans over the trapdoor.*)

TERZIANI

Do you intend to escape through that hole?

VERDI

Unless I find some tomatoes down there.

TERZIANI

A man has to earn his living.

VERDI

And to earn mine, I must return to Cairo.

He begins to lower himself through the trapdoor.

TERZIANI

I have a family to support.

VERDI

I had one. They died.

TERZIANI

I have debts.

VERDI

I got rid of mine.

TERZIANI

I have goats.

VERDI

    (*as he disappears through the trapdoor*) I
sacrificed mine.

TERZIANI

    I have mistresses. I've sold vineyards, casks,
wheelbarrows, mortar, trowels, plaster, I have
to pay for my supplies, and the people who
sow the crops say they'll have to come twice
this year, the earth is so resistant in April, my
coffers are almost empty, the throat specialists
tell me that I should consider purveying the
pleasures of the table, but if you saw the state
of my plates ... Fortunately, I'm interested in
the administration of the nation's resources
and I intend to become a shareholder, as
long as they help me.

* * * *

LA STOLZ

    (*reading a letter*) "For me, la Stolz who sang
the role of *La Favorita* is, and will always
remain, that precious haven that gives
meaning to the storm of temporary truths. La
Stolz has always been a supreme aria rising
from a wellspring whose waters contain no
despair, an angel who pretends to be unaware

32

of her power and who continues perhaps to be unaware of everything, as happiness clings to those who win at the game of ignorance. You embody my faith, my dear Teresa. I am writing from Cairo so you know that the roads of Milan are many, and I am walking one of those roads. Giuseppe Verdi."

* * * *

> *VERDI enters through the trapdoor, followed by THE PROMPTER.*

THE PROMPTER
> *In testa che avete, signor Ceprano?*
> *Ei sbuffa! Vedete?*
> *Che festa!*
> *Oh si!*
> *Il Duca qui pur si diverte!*
> *Cosi non è sempre?*
> *Il giuco ed il vino,*
> *Le feste, la danza,*
> *Battaglia, conviti,*
> *Ben tutto gli sta!*

VERDI
> Who are you?

THE PROMPTER

Exhausting endeavours, long and costly in the autumn years, fated marriage, difference in age between politics and the arts, the stage, the theatre, luxury, learning, teachers and players, the wheel of chance, Italy in all its splendour, in the eyes of the last of the buffoons contemplating the last of the kings. Who am I? Crouching beneath my trapdoor in the basement of the Opera, living in the dark by night and by day, ready to pounce when your faulty memory sends you skittering my way, who do you think I am? Rigoletto. Monterone. Delighted to meet you. Your name? Please forgive the state of my poor eyes that can no longer see beyond the dark of my hole. (*staring at VERDI*) You're not the director? You're not Minister Penco? Wait … I recognize you … Yes … that top hat, surly in your proud humility, goodnatured despite a certain stiffness, an almost military stiffness, you must be … my God … Maestro … Oh, signor Maestro! Who ever would have thought? Wait … They must've kidnapped you. They succeeded. A political strategy. This director was appointed as a result of endless intrigue. Totally corrupt. The man knows nothing about music. You'll see, he relies on Terziani's judgement. Alone, you will accomplish nothing worthwhile with him in charge. But, don't despair, no matter what happens, I'll be here. Hidden in the shadows.

Give me your hand. Feel my heart. It's the
Verdi in me. This libretto belongs to you,
lucky man. There lies your saving grace. Let
me serve you, Maestro. I'll watch your opera
take shape from here. Since I have yet to find
my way, I'll prove a busy actor in your play.
Curtain. You must start work immediately, for
your task is written in the stars.

II

The following day. The space now looks more like a rehearsal hall. One corner has been set up as a raised proscenium. Costumes and props are scattered everywhere. Downstage, the piano is strewn with pages of a manuscript score. THE PROMPTER is sitting at the piano, playing as VERDI dictates the score. VERDI is rehearsing LA STOLZ. THE DIRECTOR, still armed, is pacing back and forth.

LA STOLZ
Non pianger, mia compagna
No, le nesci il tuo dolor ...

VERDI
More slowly.

LA STOLZ
Non ... pian ... ger, mia com ... pa ... gna
No, le nes ... ci il tuo do ... lor ...

VERDI
Il tuo dolor ...

LA STOLZ
Il tuo dolor ...

THE DIRECTOR
I had a dream.

VERDI
(*to LA STOLZ*) No *rubato*.

LA STOLZ
Fine.

THE DIRECTOR
That the future was at last the present.

VERDI
(*to LA STOLZ*) The queen is bidding farewell
to her kingdom of France.

LA STOLZ
Yes, Maestro. I realize that.

THE DIRECTOR
You had just finished "Médor" and it was a
beautiful, important opera.

VERDI
There won't be any "Médor."

THE DIRECTOR
What do you mean?

VERDI
I prefer *Don Carlo*.

THE DIRECTOR
Pardon me?

VERDI
Your proposal is grotesque.

THE DIRECTOR
    You prefer …

VERDI
    Don Carlo, the son of the King of Spain.

THE DIRECTOR
    That's the title?

VERDI
    Whether you like it or not.

LA STOLZ
    Maestro, in this—

THE DIRECTOR
    Is it the same story? Penco insists that—

VERDI
    And what about Verdi?

THE DIRECTOR
    Be careful. Penco is Penco.

VERDI
    And Verdi?

THE DIRECTOR
    Of course, I'll point that out to Penco. Fine.
    Don … Don … Don whatever will do. As long
    as it serves the best interests of the nation, I'll
    lend my support. Our political ambitions are
    on the verge of transforming Italy. Minister
    Penco wept the other morning. He wept
    because he realized that an opera is

38

something sublime. The more grandiose the work, the more supportive the people. You're right, Verdi. Make it Don ... Don ...

VERDI
Don Carlo.

LA STOLZ
Could somebody please pay attention to me.

THE DIRECTOR
Penco is a great man, you know. He appointed Ermano Tozzi Brigadier of Fine Arts. Arviso, Chief Officer of Sculpture. The ex-colonel Schnupp, Theatre Commissary and Dramaturgical Consultant. And me, Gualtier Mariani, officer of the Legion of Honour, *direttore dell'opera alla Scala.*

VERDI
(*handing a sheet of music to THE DIRECTOR*) The first act is fairly straightforward. Here's the synopsis. (*to LA STOLZ who has picked up her coat and is leaving*) Where are you going?

THE DIRECTOR
Teresa Stolz, where are you going?

LA STOLZ
I'm leaving.

THE DIRECTOR
No one has the right to leave this room.

VERDI

(*to LA STOLZ*) Let's carry on.

THE DIRECTOR

(*reading the synopsis*) Why, this story is grandiose. Don Carlo and the Queen of France meet at Fontainebleau. Isn't that grandiose?

VERDI

(*to LA STOLZ*) C, A flat. Let's carry on.

LA STOLZ

Again?

VERDI

Again.

LA STOLZ

This music is too languid.

VERDI

I said, let's carry on.

LA STOLZ

It's too languid.

VERDI

What?

LA STOLZ

Meno largo. If it is really Verdi, it will be faster.

VERDI

Are you the composer?

LA STOLZ

Are you the singer? For once you're going to listen to me. (*singing*)

Non pianger, mia compagna
No, le nesci il tuo dolor.

Isn't that what you wrote, Maestro? Don't argue.

THE DIRECTOR

The two of them fall in love. How grandiose. So as not to disappoint her people, the Queen of France agrees to marry the King of Spain. And to make it even grander, she agrees despite the fact that she is engaged to the son of the King of Spain. Even more grandiose. Show me the music.

VERDI

I'm hungry. I'm thirsty.

THE DIRECTOR

When you've finished writing.

VERDI

Some ham.

THE DIRECTOR

For some ham, I want an overture.

VERDI

Some bread.

THE DIRECTOR

For some bread, a recitative. An aria for some
salad. A duet, *prosciutto e melone.*

VERDI

Here, that's an *e melone* duet.

THE DIRECTOR
What about the overture?

VERDI
No overture.

THE DIRECTOR
Then no ham.

VERDI

Seek what is true. Since *La Forza*, no more
overtures. The story should begin directly
with the main character, not with a concert.

THE DIRECTOR
Terziani, what do you think?

TERZIANI

Until there's evidence to the contrary, all
good operas begin with a display of the full
orchestra.

VERDI
Bravo, Terziani.

THE DIRECTOR
I want this display.

VERDI
You'll have it at the end.

THE DIRECTOR
Now.

VERDI
Let me finish the prologue.

THE DIRECTOR
Terziani. What's this prologue like?

TERZIANI
It's awful, Signor Mariani. At the moment, I have twelve notes to sing and la Stolz already has seventy-seven.

THE DIRECTOR
(*indicating the score*) But look, this entrance of the king who confronts the queen and can't control his jealousy, it's a dramatic gem. Are you telling me that he manages to do that in only twelve notes?

TERZIANI
Six, to be precise.

THE DIRECTOR
And the six others?

TERZIANI
The reprise. And furthermore, the accompaniment is loaded with mistakes.

THE DIRECTOR
What sort of mistakes?

TERZIANI
Harmonic mistakes.

THE DIRECTOR
I couldn't care less about that. (*to VERDI*)
Show me the scene.

> *VERDI passes several pages of the manuscript to*
> *THE DIRECTOR who glances at them while*
> *VERDI continues to rehearse LA STOLZ.*

VERDI
The Queen of France, now the wife of the
King of Spain, maintains a secret liaison with
Don Carlo, the son.

TERZIANI
The son?

VERDI
The king's son.

TERZIANI
But isn't he her son?

VERDI
Her stepson, if you wish.

TERZIANI
Her son-in-law?

VERDI
No!

TERZIANI
Isn't he her daughter's husband?

VERDI
She doesn't have a daughter, idiot.

TERZIANI
Why call me an idiot? She could have.

VERDI
Not in this context.

TERZIANI
What about this king?

VERDI
A man of power who is fond of his subjects,
who appreciates beautiful objects, authentic
furnishings and purebred animals.

TERZIANI
Perfect, I've been crazy about such animals
since I was a boy. My other passions, those
involving human beings, have never lasted
more than three days.

VERDI
Don't tell me you're as lacking in intelligence
as you are in voice.

TERZIANI
You've just said something else to belittle me.

VERDI

When they see you in the role of Philip II, the men in the audience will stop envying those who are kings.

THE DIRECTOR

(*handing the manuscript back to VERDI*) It makes no sense at all.

TERZIANI

(*to THE DIRECTOR*) And the story is only beginning.

THE DIRECTOR

Verdi, you'll have to make it simpler. There was nothing complicated about the libretto I gave you. Why did you have to change the title and the content? You must create a work that the people can understand.

VERDI

A work that will keep the people in a state of delusion.

THE DIRECTOR

Your job is to entertain them.

VERDI

Don Carlo is not a circus.

THE DIRECTOR

Nor is the Treaty we have signed. Such an uncooperative attitude is tantamount to a refusal, a revival of the debate on the most controversial points of the Treaty, perhaps even the minister's resignation, and the collapse of the Party. You expect me to show this to Penco? This? This? You call this ... music? This is supposed to usher in the future? (*He tears up the sheets of music in front of a devastated VERDI.*) Our adversaries are working day and night. They know what the people want to hear. A rebellion is brewing. The masses are grumbling. If we get tangled up in an ambiguous opera nobody can understand, if the high point of the festivities heralding the new regime proves to be a failure, who will ever believe in the importance of Unification? Time is of the essence. (*aiming his revolver*) Maestro Giuseppe Verdi, you have thirty-six hours left to write me an opera, with five acts, a prologue, a full orchestral overture, complete with chorus and ballet. I promised a grandiose opera, I want a grandiose opera.

* * * *

LA STOLZ
(*reading a letter from VERDI*) "I am writing from Cairo, more smitten with you than with any

other cantatrice, than with music itself, when I rise at dawn to face operas which do not allay my fears. I relive yesterday's triumphs and ask myself whether tomorrow will bring them anew. Those of today beckon, like days to be relived, more crucial than the past, for the past held neither the pain nor the faith in the love I have for Teresa. Do I dare believe that tomorrow will be made of a more vehement today, as I anticipate the colossal opera that the interminable Egyptian negotiations hold in store for me farther east? I am referring to everything that speaks to me and I speak to myself: I am Giuseppe Verdi, but what good does it do?"

VERDI moves closer to LA STOLZ.

LA STOLZ
Indeed, what good does it do, if you sent the same letter to all my rivals? If, while the Nile flows in its bed, la Benza reads these same sentences before falling asleep in hers?

* * * *

Introduction to Act III of Don Carlo. *THE PROMPTER is accompanying the aria on the*

piano. TERZIANI, in the role of Philip II of
Spain, is giving his recitative:

TERZIANI
> *Ella giammai m'amò*
> *No, quel cor chiuso m'è*
> *Amor per me non ha*
> *Per me non ha.*
>
> *He pauses.*
>
> But look at the end … *Che Dio sol può*
> *veder …*

THE PROMPTER
> "That God alone can see."

TERZIANI
> God … On the highest note.

THE PROMPTER
> God?
>
> *He stops playing.*

TERZIANI
> I'm just a humble baritone. There's a legend
> that says … when a singer has trouble hitting
> the highest note in his aria, the composer
> returns from the hereafter, he stands in the
> shadows and with one withering look he will
> strike down the man who failed in his duty—

THE PROMPTER
> It's true.

TERZIANI
How do you know?

THE PROMPTER
I know.

TERZIANI
Have you seen many apparitions?

THE PROMPTER
Quite a few.

TERZIANI
And what does the composer say?

THE PROMPTER
It all depends.

TERZIANI
Upon what?

THE PROMPTER
What he ate for supper.

TERZIANI
Can everyone on stage hear him?

THE PROMPTER
Everyone close to the singer.

TERZIANI
Have you personally heard composers speak
to those singers?

THE PROMPTER
Occasionally.

TERZIANI
Which ones?

THE PROMPTER
(*searching*) Bellini.

TERZIANI
And seeing the composers haunt the singers, doesn't it terrify you?

THE PROMPTER
Why? I'm used to it. Besides, I'm the last one who'd be surprised to see them appear to the tune of words I am the first to say, words I've been saying for ages. I often feel as if I am summoning ghosts. "*Casta diva*" … Imagine! The curtain has just risen, and the minute they appear, those poor cantatrices who can barely control their stagefright have to sing either a B flat or a straight B or a high C … "*Casta diva* … " I've seen Bellini taking stock more often than I've seen Norma succeed. The composer appears in the shadows, looking distressed, since he feels contrite about terrifying men and women for centuries to come, simply because he couldn't resist the temptation of applying ink to a space just a touch above the scale, without even straining his fingers. Now he must pay for the power he possessed in his lifetime. The power to make souls swoon in a single, dizzying instant, but also the power to snap the vocal cords of the greatest in the

world of opera, Mercadante, Colonnese, Benza, poor Teresa Stolz! All would rather die forgotten than find themselves on stage stranded in their own silence. That's why the composer reappears to offer a word of consolation, first to them, then to himself. Sometimes the distraught eyes of this strange couple come to rest on the floor whose boards sustain my own gaze, and I have seen vast deserts swept by more remorse contained in art than art contains ambition. Remorse is sand and triumph an oasis. The tearful eyes of the composer and his singer seek in mine the mirror of their grief, a glimmer of comprehension, a vague sense of compassion ... but I am only the prompter. I can offer no tears to reflect theirs. My eyes are as dry as an insomniac's, because they remain rivetted to the tiny lines of the libretto! What if I were to fail in my duty! Here I am, a humble hunchback, and shortsighted at that, so nothing I have witnessed has taken place beyond the tip of my nose. I have seen Isolde die beneath my gaze, but I've seen nothing of her love for Tristan, nor of the sea and sky. I have seen Don Juan perish countless times, but I've never been able to admire the extravagance of his feast. Bah, what's the point? Who cares about my complaints? I am an ignorant prompter in charge of the words but not the tone. My task is simply to deliver the words to others, knowing that someone

else will promptly say them better. I accepted
long ago to whisper in the dark words I would
have preferred to save for myself, instead of
listening to their echo reverberate for the
multitude. Oh, woe unto him who claims that
a libretto is a mediocre thing, for that is
where I have drawn the very stuff of my
knowledge. I would have gladly remained
ignorant of passion; I'd be the first to say that
love is a sham. There is no work more
thankless than mine. There's no sense in
dreaming of promotions—what future is
there for a prompter? Where can someone go
who has spent his life in a hole? Whispering
words would be frowned upon under any
other circumstances, and aside from those
who try to cure the mad, who would be
interested in me? The conductor? He ignores
me. I am the only one he can't see. The
opera directors? They come and go without
ever realizing that great things have small
beginnings. Very small. *Pianissimo.* Then,
from *pianissimo* to *piano,* and from *piano* to
mezzo forte, and from *forte* to *più forte,* and then
fortissimo … si, comè un colpo di canòne. You
know, given all the contrived anguish and all
the deaths that take place here before my
very eyes, and since it is true, for you as well
as for me, that everything is feasible and all
manner of apparition possible, to answer your
question, Rinuccio Terziani, no, oh no, the

resurrection of those who imagined all this is
not about to terrify me.

* * * *

LA STOLZ
Venice is alive with a thousand and one
Verdis. They come and go all around me,
until I'm ready to surrender to the first, then
the second, provided he says that his name is
Giuseppe Verdi.

VERDI
For every Verdi at the Carnival, there was a
woman who claimed to be Italy's greatest
cantatrice. Even la Benza was disguised as
Teresa Stolz. Yet I never doubted that the real
Teresa Stolz was you.

LA STOLZ
Perhaps, but how was I to know who I was
speaking to? Another man just before you
had spent ten minutes swearing his name was
Verdi.

VERDI
Why didn't you leave with him?

LA STOLZ

Perhaps I did. In which case, I am speaking to that man now.

VERDI

You are speaking to me now. I told you my name. You believed me. Because I am Verdi.

LA STOLZ

I was surrounded by as many doubts as there were Verdis in Venice that night. But we agreed to leave our doubts and look-alikes outside the bedroom door. Though they reappeared afterwards. The minute I set foot outside the hotel that morning, I saw a small group of Verdis singing *La donna è mobile*. And they were all pointing their fingers at me. I was the one who felt like the woman in the song, the woman who flits from one man to another. And you, the man I had just left behind, who were you?

VERDI

Those men had spent the night drinking and singing under our window. They were as drunk as we were.

LA STOLZ

You were drunk.

VERDI

What about you? You weren't drunk? At the foot of the stairs, were you sober?

LA STOLZ

Verdi might have been one of the men
singing and pointing their fingers at me.

VERDI

Then who might I have been?

LA STOLZ

You instead of another, by mere chance.

VERDI

But that night, the man you slept with was
me. The woman was you.

LA STOLZ

But in the morning, when I found myself
alone in the street, the Verdi in my head was
so great he had once again become
impossible in real life. The man I had loved
seemed to be multiplied by a hundred.

VERDI

Not one of them could have talked about
Aida the way I did while making love.

LA STOLZ

I was Stolz's wife and I had made love with
another man.

VERDI

You asked me I don't know how many times
for proof that I was the one and only. You
made me sing silly arias, intrigues I am
ashamed to have composed. I begged you to

stop. But you kept asking for more. What was
I supposed to do?

LA STOLZ

Take me away with you.

VERDI

I asked you to come with me, but there was
Stolz.

LA STOLZ

Stay at my side.

VERDI

There was Stolz.

LA STOLZ

Prevent the others from being Verdi.

VERDI

Is it my fault that all the men of Venice,
except for Stolz, were disguised as Verdi?

LA STOLZ

Who keeps sending these notes from Cairo
full of promises to one woman after another?
A love letter is not an opera written for all of
Italy.

VERDI

I'd like to burn all those letters.

LA STOLZ

You once wanted to burn *Nabucco*.

VERDI

Because the melody of the Hebrew chorus—

LA STOLZ

Made you sick to your stomach. Perhaps I
have a match in my purse so you can burn all
the passions you conceive! This *Don Carlo* you
are in the process of writing, and *Aida* which
you have promised to us all, to me la Stolz,
and to la Benza, la Garibaldi, la Strepponi
and la Ventadour—

VERDI

Oh no, not to her.

LA STOLZ

She admires you as much as the others. What
difference does it make? Sooner or later, all
of us will make you sick to your stomach.

VERDI

Why don't you all write the opera that suits
you! You can write the total Verdi. And if your
opera doesn't meet with Penco's satisfaction,
he'll simply have to find someone else. They
have polluted Venice. Now Milan has
succumbed. There's nothing left for me here.
I'll go and contaminate Cairo.

LA STOLZ

No!

VERDI
Too anonymous in Venice, too famous in Milan. My true place is in Egypt, beside the Sphinx.

LA STOLZ
Verdi!

She kisses him.

VERDI
Now what should we do?

LA STOLZ
Leave for Cairo. I want to sail the seas with you, embrace the beckoning horizon. I want the voyage to transport us, I want to feel the storms swell and the deck fall beneath our feet. You will hold me tight near the rigging, in the din of the engines, the smell of rust and the sigh of the wind.

VERDI
I love you, Teresa.

They kiss.

LA STOLZ
Giuseppe Verdi!

VERDI
Now do you want to tear off Verdi's beard and wig? Remove the mask and grease paint and see the Verdi hidden underneath?

* * * *

THE DIRECTOR

    I had another dream. Ever since I've been in
Culture, I have two dreams a day. There was a
halo over Minister Penco's head, a halo of
unearthly whiteness. In the distance, a
flourish of trumpets, choirs, the Choral
Society and the ambassadors. The pristine
morning sparkled as if the sun was a mere
ornament in the midst of the banquet, and
the national opera, escorted by immaculate
horsemen, proved at last, yes, at last, to be
more total and more divine than the Church.
Maestro Giuseppe Verdi, you have twenty-four
hours left.

* * * *

TERZIANI

    "Non una dama almeno presso di voi serbaste?"

VERDI

    "Not one among your retinue attended to her
duty?"

60

TERZIANI
"Nota non v'è la legge mia regal?"

VERDI
"Do you not know what royal law demands?"
With more authority, Terziani.

TERZIANI
"Quale dama d'onor ... "

THE DIRECTOR
With more authority, Terziani. You heard
maestro Verdi.

TERZIANI
"Quale dama d'onor esser dovea con voi?"

VERDI
Which one? Who should have been there?
Who disobeyed? Which one?

LA STOLZ
Excuse me.

THE DIRECTOR
Silence.

LA STOLZ
I have something to ask you.

VERDI
(*losing patience*) Not now.

LA STOLZ
(*insulted*) What?

VERDI

(*brusquely*) I said not now.

LA STOLZ

Basta! (*She slaps him.*) I'm asking for a
moment of respite.

THE DIRECTOR

The libretto! The libretto!

TERZIANI

Don't tell me you're going to contest such a
perfect pretext for an aria!

LA STOLZ

What glory is there in triumph if nobody can
feel my discomfort?

VERDI

We do feel it.

LA STOLZ

(*brusquely, to VERDI*) Be quiet! (*miserable, to
TERZIANI and THE DIRECTOR*) I can't
concentrate, and I can't bear having the two
of you stare at me.

TERZIANI

You disobeyed the king. A page of virtuosity is
bound to follow. Can't you handle it?

LA STOLZ

I neglected to tend to a duty, and now I am
paying for it dearly.

THE DIRECTOR
Nonsense, *Madame la Stolz*. That's not in keeping with the temperament of the Queen of Spain. You must stand up to the king in all your dignity.

LA STOLZ
As a cantatrice, queen or not, I'm suffering from a discomfort that prevents me from singing.

TERZIANI
I have some lozenges.

LA STOLZ
I would like permission to leave the room briefly, Signor Mariani.

THE DIRECTOR
That is forbidden.

LA STOLZ
My reasons are crucial.

TERZIANI
La Stolz, indisposed?

THE DIRECTOR
No more tête-à-têtes with the maestro.

LA STOLZ
That's not the point.

TERZIANI
What is it then?

THE DIRECTOR
Your lungs?

TERZIANI
Your throat?

LA STOLZ
Neither my lungs nor my throat.

TERZIANI
Higher than that?

THE DIRECTOR
Mal'alla testa?

LA STOLZ
Lower.

TERZIANI
The diaphragm?

LA STOLZ
I—

THE DIRECTOR
Your stomach?

LA STOLZ
I need—

THE DIRECTOR
Now what do you need?

LA STOLZ
I need to pee.

THE DIRECTOR
  Oh! (*Beat.*) No. The answer is no! Over the
  past few hours, I've allowed each of you to
  withdraw to the wings, and most of the time
  there was absolutely no need for it. You
  claimed you had to relieve yourselves, one
  after the other, whenever you pleased, you,
  Terziani, at five to midnight, and before that
  at quarter to midnight, and before that at
  twenty to midnight.

VERDI
  You can't refuse, it's her right.

  *THE DIRECTOR places a chamber pot in the
  middle of the stage to everyone's stupefaction.*

THE DIRECTOR
  (*turning to LA STOLZ*) Look upon this
  inconvenience as a kind of Lent you must
  observe for Verdi, until Minister Penco's
  dawn rises like Easter Morning.

VERDI
  (*turns to attack THE DIRECTOR*) *Cane rognoso!*

  THE DIRECTOR points his gun at VERDI.

THE DIRECTOR
  Cane rognoso a chi?

VERDI
  Sudicia palla di lardo! (*turning to LA STOLZ*)
  No, Teresa! I forbid you!

LA STOLZ steps out of her panties, walks over to the pot, lifts her skirts and sits down. A long silence. Then she gestures discreetly to THE PROMPTER who sits down at the piano. LA STOLZ's voice fills the room.

LA STOLZ

Non pianger, mia compagna,
Non pianger no,
Le nesci il tuo dolor.
Bandita sei di Spagna
Ma non da questo cor.
Con te del viver mio
Fu lieta l'alba ancor
Ritorna al suo nati,
Ti seguira il mio cor,
Ah! Te seguira il mio cor.

VERDI grabs the revolver and aims it at THE DIRECTOR. Blackout. Gunshot.

* * * *

THE DIRECTOR
(*wounded*) My dear Penco, my life is coming to an end, so soon, shattered beyond repair. All that remains is a tale of opera management and heroics in these ruins, so

that Italy, our beloved Italy, might play the heroine. I will have watched the night unfold in the uninspired neutrality of treaties, with no hope of dawn, because the next opera will be made of a great hammering, and ignorance will continue to precipitate us into opera after opera after opera. The support of our faithful Terziani, sole and constant source of enlightenment, beacon of comprehension and rigour, will have provided some consolation for the only possible truth: I fear that maestro Giuseppe Verdi, rather than mastering the labyrinth, constitutes its beginning and its end.

III

*Late at night. Atmosphere of confusion reigns
on stage. Costumes, props, as well as the
personal belongings of TERZIANI, VERDI and
LA STOLZ are scattered everywhere. Everything
is topsy-turvy. Manuscript pages lie everywhere,
covering the piano and the floor around it.
Dawn is approaching. Exhausted, THE
PROMPTER and VERDI are gathering up pages
and reconstituting the score of* Don Carlo.

THE PROMPTER

You are a free man, Maestro. (*Beat.*) What are
you going to do with *Don Carlo*?

VERDI

To hell with Minister Penco and his opera.

THE PROMPTER

How can you say that? (*thumbing through the
pages of the score, distressed*) Look … you have
never written anything more beautiful than
this aria for the King of Spain.

VERDI

I have never written anything so bad.

THE PROMPTER

You can't abandon this opera.

VERDI

They're expecting me in Cairo. I must return, especially since I have done what I came here to do.

THE PROMPTER

Do you mean you intended to write *Don Carlo?*

VERDI

I came to see la Stolz again.

THE PROMPTER

But I will never see you again. A great opera was taking shape before my very eyes, and now you tell me I will never see it finished? I beg of you, Maestro, stay. In the name of the Verdi in me. (*He sits down at the piano and plays several notes. Insistently, in tears.*) How can you leave this music unfinished? Do you really think that this F sharp ... If we were to change the key signature ... listen ... (*He plays the same bars in another key.*) Listen ... That's Verdi at his greatest.

> *He plays the aria,* Dormirò sol. *TERZIANI enters.*

VERDI

How is he?

TERZIANI

His arm has stopped bleeding. He fell asleep.

VERDI

> Don't wake him.

TERZIANI

> (*walking over to the piano, in a melancholy tone*)
> And what will become of me now, will I go
> back to the way I was? Drifting downstream
> like a log on the river? Verdi composing an
> opera before my eyes, that at least was
> something.

VERDI

> You'll wait for the minister, and you'll tell him
> what you witnessed.

TERZIANI

> What if he asks us to play the opera for him?

VERDI

> Then you'll have to play it.

> *LA STOLZ enters, wearing a cloak.*

LA STOLZ

> I'm ready, Maestro.

VERDI

> And so am I, Teresa.

LA STOLZ

> No, Verdi. I am leaving. But you must stay.
> When the minister's henchmen kidnapped
> me as I left the theatre, I offered no
> resistance. It was an unexpected opportunity
> to see you again. I didn't know whether the

Verdi I was going to see would be the man from Venice. Well, it was.

VERDI
You are free. I am free.

LA STOLZ
We will be free once you've finished the opera that all of Italy is waiting for.

VERDI
Go on writing for Penco?

LA STOLZ
For Teresa Stolz. If it is true that since Venice you only write for me, you must finish your work. I know that sooner or later, if you don't finish *Don Carlo*, it will always be my fault in your eyes. But I won't allow that. I must be the one who begs you to write to the end.

VERDI
Don Carlo is almost finished.

LA STOLZ
What about the last act?

VERDI
Give me another half hour and you'll have it.

LA STOLZ
One cannot finish a total work of art in a half hour. That *Non Pianger* is just a nursery rhyme. Lacking in surprise, without innovation. You must start over again, Verdi.

VERDI
Start over again—

LA STOLZ
I don't expect any promises, or any letters.
(*She places the letters from Cairo on the piano.*) I
am leaving the way I stepped out of the
gondola in Venice, telling myself that the
man behind me was Verdi.

VERDI
What about the others? Those who will
appear ahead of you?

LA STOLZ
Not if I leave before daybreak, while they are
still sleeping. (*fragile*) Please, don't wake
them.

* * * *

THE PROMPTER
(*intrigued*) Maestro ... these letters.

VERDI
They belong to me.

THE PROMPTER

They were mailed from Cairo. (*He compares the letters and the score.*) You didn't write them.

VERDI

Those are my words ...

THE PROMPTER

But it's not your handwriting.

> *VERDI grabs the letters from him and tears them up violently.*

VERDI

These letters do not exist.

THE PROMPTER

They exist. And *Don Carlo* exists.

VERDI

No!

THE PROMPTER

Someone signed these letters in Verdi's name.

VERDI

(*as he continues to destroy the letters frantically*) Another impostor. Yet another. Just one? Of course not! There are hundreds of them, thousands!

THE PROMPTER

(*grabbing a fragment, reading*) "You and only you, Teresa Stolz ... "

VERDI

Stop! Those words are like a waterfall
thundering through a gorge, a strident noise
I heard between her and me, the minute she
showed me those letters. There are so many
Verdis between us, who have no time, no age,
no hour, no tale to tell.

He heads toward the door.

THE PROMPTER

(*assertively*) Where are you going?

VERDI

To join her.

THE PROMPTER

She'll be back.

VERDI

La Stolz! Teresa Stolz has gone.

THE PROMPTER

If you really are Giuseppe Verdi, she'll come
back.

VERDI

What do you mean?

THE PROMPTER

If I were Giuseppe Verdi, I'd be sure she'd
come back.

VERDI

(*overwhelmed*) A million Verdis. When they
appear, the hunt begins: I chase them, they
maintain their lead. But suddenly they spin
around and I must confront them. And to my
surprise, I am the one to flee, for they
outnumber me.

*He sits down at the piano and lets his head
fall onto the keyboard. THE PROMPTER
approaches, picks the revolver up from where it
was lying among the scattered pages and slowly
points the gun at VERDI.*

THE PROMPTER

Maestro, you must carry on with your work.

*Beat. VERDI is startled, both frightened and
surprised.*

VERDI

But … why?

THE PROMPTER

For the Verdi in me.

VERDI

There is no one in you but a sewer rat.

THE PROMPTER

For the Verdi I am.

VERDI

That would make you one among hundreds, thousands of others. Enough of this! I am dead tired.

THE PROMPTER

But since I am Giuseppe Verdi.

VERDI

And perhaps you're the minister, why not?

THE PROMPTER

No, I'm not the minister. But I am Giuseppe Verdi.

VERDI

Get out of here.

THE PROMPTER

I'd love to leave for Cairo, of course. But I can't. Because we have to finish *Don Carlo* together, you and I.

VERDI

Get out of here.

THE PROMPTER

Now you. Now you don't believe me. It must be because I'm too humble. Nobody believes me. Yet I carry here in my heart the suffering of the oppressed, and the vanity of kings. Yes, I've behaved like a rat, a rat who observes the world from below. I've been obeying you for the past thirty-six hours. Servile, bowing and

scraping, agreeing with everything you say
and everything you are. There is no Verdi
more faithful than I.

VERDI

Who are you?

THE PROMPTER

I told you, Giuseppe Verdi. Who do you want
me to be? Amonasro?

VERDI

Amonasro?

THE PROMPTER

Ma tu re, o signore possente … But how can I
sing the role of Amonasro, since you haven't
published *Aida* yet … ? *Rigoletto? La donna è
mobile* … Yes, your greatest triumph. *In testa
che avete?* I know it all by heart, and small
wonder. Who am I? Italy in all its splendour,
in the eyes of the last of the buffoons
contemplating the last of the kings … I am
just a traveller. Who, like you, arrived on a
train from Cairo, here to see Teresa Stolz
again. An opera composer being held
hostage, like you, in la Scala in Milan. I am
alone. I'm talking to you, but it's to myself. La
Stolz has gone, and I am alone. With a
solitude that adds to my misery. And if there
were a hundred of us, it would make no
difference. Instead of a duet, there would be
a chorus. A chorus without voices. An opera

without music. We would be alone, horribly alone. Without light, without form. Ocean without water, desert without sand. The grandest set the emptiest mind could conceive.

THE PROMPTER removes his hunchback, his wig, his false nose and proves to be in every way identical to VERDI, who has frozen on the spot.

* * * *

Two VERDIs stand facing each other. VERDI I grabs the revolver and points it at VERDI II (THE PROMPTER).

VERDI I
   Who are you?

VERDI II
   Verdi. Pleased to meet you. And you?

VERDI I
   Who am I?

VERDI II
   Who are you?

VERDI I

I …

VERDI II

Put down your weapon. (*He picks up the
revolver and aims it at the score of* Don Carlo.)
There are harmonic mistakes in our opera.

VERDI I

It's because I have so little time.

VERDI II

Because I write first, and I correct afterwards.
Really, didn't anyone teach you the difference
between an F double sharp and a G? Between
a C flat and a B? Between a prelude, a mere
introduction and an overture?

VERDI I

No, no overture. Since *La Forza*, no more
overtures. The true drama should begin with
the characters, with no embellishment. This
obsession with wanting to be me makes you a
despicable bandit. Your disguises are
grotesque.

VERDI II

(*taking aim*) And you are sordid. Imitating my
signature like that. You could find yourself
behind bars.

VERDI I

Where have you come from?

VERDI II
Cairo.

VERDI I
The name of the ship?

VERDI II
The Ramses.

VERDI I
The name of the train?

VERDI II
The Palatino.

VERDI I
The time of your arrival?

VERDI II
Eight o'clock at night.

VERDI I
On time?

VERDI II
Yes, for once.

VERDI I
Anyone could check on that.

VERDI II
Including the people who took you hostage
and mistook you for me.

VERDI I

A *Masked Ball,* Act III, Scene II, seventh measure, eighth note?

A quarter of a second.

VERDI II

B flat.

VERDI I

Your papers.

VERDI II

What right do you have?

VERDI I

Your papers.

> *VERDI II hands over his papers. VERDI I glances at them.*

VERDI II

Born in le Roncole.

VERDI I

Marriage certificate. With my own wife.

VERDI II

My wife and children died more than twenty years ago.

VERDI I

And my visa for Egypt. What's this supposed to mean?

VERDI II

That my presence in Egypt is necessary for the success of *Aida*.

VERDI I

Then why would you have come here?

VERDI II

Thief! You've stolen my score.

VERDI I

Answer me.

VERDI II

I came to compose *Don Carlo*. How can you have it in your possession?

VERDI I

Do you often lose your masterpieces?

VERDI II

That opera is worthless, you said so yourself.

VERDI I

"This is great Verdi." Those were your own words.

VERDI II

Only a few pages. And those pages belong to me.

They struggle. The revolver rolls on the ground, then VERDI I picks it up.

VERDI I

(*aiming the revolver*) That's enough.

VERDI II

It's my head. It's my heart. My soul.

VERDI I

That's enough.

VERDI II

Everything I've written will remain after I am gone. Even if you pull the trigger.

VERDI I

And if I do?

VERDI II

I shall remain myself. Intact with all my memories. My memory might have confused the dates, the weddings and births, the deaths, but certain details remain, never to be erased. My first love …

VERDI I

(*aiming the gun*) Your first love?

VERDI II

In Busseto.

VERDI I

Too obvious.

VERDI II

Her name was Maria Angelina.

VERDI I

    I know a dozen women with that name.

VERDI II

    Maria Angelina Tozzi.

VERDI I

    Was she angelic?

VERDI II

    She wasn't even pretty. But as a child, I felt an inexplicable love for her. I found it so disturbing, I never dared mention it to anyone.

VERDI I

    …

VERDI II

    She had a slight limp, and I was afraid people would make fun of me.

VERDI I

    …

VERDI II

    And that's why, when she died, I missed my music class, and I tried to kill myself.

VERDI I

    That's enough.

VERDI II

    I was six years old and I had only one desire: to die.

VERDI I

I never wanted to die.

VERDI II

Remember, you were drunk in Venice, the day after the night you spent with Teresa Stolz, and deep down inside, you had only one desire.

VERDI I

(*about to pull the trigger*) To see her again.

VERDI II

To die!

> *VERDI I aims the gun at VERDI II.*

* * * *

> *VERDI II is holding the gun.*

VERDI I

None of this ... tell me ... none of this is true. The phenomenon is possible, but none of it is true.

VERDI II

You're trembling? That's a good sign. When the earth trembles, the mountains move closer to each other.

VERDI I

Enough nonsense. Opera leads us into the worst labyrinths.

VERDI II

That which would appear to be false …

VERDI I

Remains false. If we could always perceive the truth with perfect clarity, we wouldn't have to spend our entire lives searching for it. Neither you, the city rat, nor I the country rat.

VERDI II

Who would have thought that I could travel so far, only to meet someone who resembles me so closely? Everything fits. Even your handwriting, which is in every way identical to mine.

VERDI I

Do you really believe that if you kill me, nothing will prevent you from parading around Milan with my manuscripts?

VERDI II

You're going to give them back to me.

VERDI I

As if I should simply abandon my *Traviata*.

VERDI II

Give me back my *Traviata*.

VERDI I

And my *Don Carlo*.

VERDI II

And my *Don Carlo*.

VERDI I

And what else?

VERDI II

My faith …

VERDI I

Yes. Your faith.

VERDI II

In the absolute.

VERDI I

Meaning?

VERDI II

You have retreated so far you no longer know who you are.

VERDI I

I am Giuseppe Verdi. Born in Busseto. The only one who can know things about me the rest of the world will never know. My fears, my doubts. My most intimate thoughts at the time of my greatest triumphs. I am the one who composed *Rigoletto*. And *Aida* and *Don Carlo*.

VERDI II
Prove it.

VERDI I
...

VERDI II
(*holding the revolver to the temple of VERDI I*) Sit down at the piano.

VERDI I
You don't really think—

VERDI II
Sit down at the piano.

> *Armed, VERDI II forces VERDI I to sit down at the piano.*

VERDI I
I've always been a mediocre pianist.

VERDI II
C, D, G sharp, with the right tempo, if you really are Giuseppe Verdi, I want to hear it.

VERDI I
When Anna Celia gave me piano lessons, I couldn't take my eyes off her bosom, and I wasn't thinking about music.

VERDI II

Play!

VERDI I

I preferred playing in the fields. I hated piano. The evening of my first recital, I vomited, I vomited in public. In front of Anna Celia who had such high hopes for me. Do you want to make me vomit now?

VERDI II

(*prepared to pull the trigger*) Play!

VERDI I

Give me a cello, violin, flute and oboe, the brass, a percussion section, the full orchestra. Anything but the piano.

VERDI II

Play!

* * * *

Music. VERDI II is sitting at the piano and VERDI I is holding the gun.

VERDI I

(*in a voice that drowns the music*) More lyrical. *Sostenuto.* No, that's no way to play Verdi. In tempo. Where is the drama? What has become of the drama? ... More *brio*. C, D, G sharp. Again. Louder. *Che Dio sol può veder.* Ah ha! Garbage. What you're playing is a pale imitation of who I am. What have you done to the Neapolitan sixths? And the secondary themes? You claim to be Verdi? That God alone can see? Nonsense! As if we should believe everything you say. My dear Verdi, it's not enough to want to be Verdi.

> *VERDI II collapses. VERDI I is still threatening him with the revolver.*

VERDI II
Why do you treat me like an enemy? You're going to need me.

VERDI I
One of the two of us must die now.

VERDI II
Close your eyes. You have killed me. Open them. You died.

VERDI I
I am alive.

VERDI II
You died, but with Teresa.

VERDI I
No.

VERDI II
    A burst of light …

VERDI I
    No.

VERDI II
    That gives birth to sound soaring above its
    own echo.

VERDI I
    Teresa!

VERDI II
    Her life, an aria …

VERDI I
    Those words on your lips!

VERDI II
    Everything else an illusion.

VERDI I
    (*distraught*) You came for her. Shut up. Go
    away. Two Verdis, if you wish. But not one in
    this world—

VERDI II
    —who could share

VERDI I
    —the love

VERDI II
    —I have

91

VERDI I

   … for Teresa. I don't know why you've come here . What I do know is that I've paid dearly for that kiss from la Stolz. If it's the truth you're looking for, you are wasting your time. If it's my death, be brief.

VERDI II

I was in my hole. Composing in the shadows. But I was spying on you and la Stolz. You, the man everyone praises, more powerful than Penco, the man the entire country is watching. (*Beat.*) In Venice. On the narrow canal. I recognized her, Teresa Stolz. I was in the gondola. And I saw the look in her eyes. From the very first moment, there was love between her and me. Now Teresa Stolz's departure makes you feel so sad, you could die. Yet you must obey her. Finish *Don Carlo*. But how, without her and without me? Remember the night you had to finish *The Masked Ball*. The rehearsals were scheduled to start the following day, and the final scene was no more than a sketch. The ball scene. Nothing. Not the slightest idea. You could think of nothing but your worries. Money, house, bad weather for the crops. Ricordi was threatening you with bankruptcy if you didn't finish your opera. The later it got, the more pressing your worries became, and your *Masked Ball* seemed to contain less and less ball. Then, suddenly, the music came like a thunderbolt, the brass rang out with astounding force. Have you forgotten the miracle? Don't you remember your visitor? Less than forty-eight hours ago, a man took you hostage, threatening you at gunpoint. How can you write under such circumstances? Forty-eight hours to compose an opera ... (*He shows him the manuscript.*) Impossible, you say? Come now, Maestro, there are harmonic mistakes in our opera. Inevitable, since we have so little time. But we have an hour left? A half hour? A quarter hour?

VERDI I

A total work of art ... in so little time?

VERDI II

Time, Maestro? *In testa che avete? Tu che le vanità ... Che Dio sol può veder.* Back to work.

VERDI I

(*transfigured, returning to the libretto*) "Am I standing before the king?" (*Both VERDIs sit down at the piano.*) *Don Carlo*, Act III, the Grand Inquisitor scene. Philip II of Spain: "Yes. I bade you come here. Carlo has plunged my heart into despair and sadness. He even drew his sword against his royal father."

As VERDI II plays the scene on the piano, VERDI I puts THE PROMPTER's cloak over his shoulders. Then he sits down beside him and composes. In the gathering darkness, they look like a single man.

* * * *

TERZIANI enters.

TERZIANI

Members of the Opposition have begun to gather outside, on the steps of la Scala. Things are getting out of hand. The crowd is angry. They've heard that you are back in Milan. Citizens who came to demand that Penco resign are waiting for you to speak to them.

VERDI I

I have nothing to say to them.

TERZIANI

They don't understand why you are collaborating with Penco. You were their only hope. They say you have betrayed them.

VERDI II

Can't you see that I have work to do?

TERZIANI

> (*listening to the music*) Maestro, that music …
> How to describe such perfect symmetry?
> Those chords … It sounds like a lament rising
> from the bowels of the earth. Like the end of
> heaven and the universe.

VERDI I

> Go outside. Tell them they have to wait.

VERDI II

> I need more time to finish my opera.

TERZIANI

> But afterwards, will you speak to them?

VERDI I

> Later.

TERZIANI

> Is everything up to me? Do I have to arrange
> everything? Barely forty-eight hours ago, you
> saw me as some obscure stranger, an
> unknown baritone, everyone's humble
> servant, at the mercy of your whims. No one
> notices me, except to reproach my lack of
> voice, my lack of intelligence. But you will
> always need Rinuccio Terziani, if not to grant
> him the authority of the king of Spain, then
> to demand his obedience. If only to
> reestablish your own loyalty to the people,
> Maestro. I'll do as you ask, to keep them
> quiet, and I'm the one who'll address them,
> since I have something to say. I want you to

95

know that there are two Terzianis. One of
them is nourished by song, the other eats
whatever he finds in his bowl. When I sing,
art comes first, opera and perpetuity. When I
speak, it's the citizen expressing himself, the
good citizen among his peers, who has been
asked to do his share—I accept to do
whatever is necessary for national unity. The
man lacking in talent will speak his mind to
the people and will leave around noon to eat.
Who cares if the crowd is unhappy. I shall
console myself. One man is as true as the
other. No matter what our creditors say.

* * * *

VERDI I
> *Don Carlo.* Last act. A page of heavenly music.
> Note to Teresa Stolz. "This music will contain
> everything I feel about my destiny. Our
> destiny."

VERDI II
> A minor. A major.

VERDI I
> Which man will she choose …

VERDI II
    She appears, dressed in mourning …

VERDI I
    No, not yet. Let me hear the reprise. The
    chords in unison. I want a great display. A
    prelude … *Crescendo* … Yes … with even more
    passion.

VERDI II
    Don't hold back.

VERDI I
    Which man …

VERDI II
    What does she say?

VERDI I
    The Queen of Spain walks over to the tomb
    and contemplates the immensity of Escorial.

VERDI II
    What does she say? The libretto! What does
    she say?

VERDI I
    Which man will she choose …

VERDI II
    She enters and prostrates herself before
    Charles V's tomb. *Tu che le vanità* … "You who
    spurned all the might which the world has to
    offer … "

VERDI I

    Largo, now *piano* … more expressive … "Who found eternal peace in this tomb … "

    The music swells. The orchestra covers both VERDI I's voice and the piano music of VERDI II.

IV

*The curtain rises on the mainstage at la Scala
as TERESA STOLZ enters, dressed in the
costume of the Queen of Spain. It is the
beginning of the last act of* Don Carlo.

LA STOLZ
(*singing*)
*Tu che le vanità
Conoscesti del mondo
E godi nell'avel
Il riposo profondo,
S'ancor si piange in cielo
Piangi sul mio dolor
E porta il pianto mio
Al trono del Signor.*

VERDI I
Teresa!

He throws himself into her arms.

LA STOLZ
They've gathered outside by the hundreds on
the steps of la Scala. The entire population of
Milan has placed its fate in the hands of a
single man, and from now on their future
depends upon Verdi. I was walking in the
crowd, not knowing where I belonged. The

crowd, what a strange tentacle … It surrounds
me when I walk, stares at me when I'm on
stage, drinks in my voice when I sing. I dream
of being alone with one man, but instead I
am always alone with a thousand men and
women. Those men and women were
chanting the syllables of your name. The
musician, the genius and the idol, a man
whom I love and who once desired me. I too
have chosen. And I belong here.

VERDI I
My opera is almost finished. I love you. This
nightmare is almost over. And we can leave
together.

LA STOLZ
What about the minister?

VERDI I
I'll take you to le Roncole.

LA STOLZ
Yes. Le Roncole.

VERDI I
Busseto, the magnolias. Far from Milan, far
from the crowds.

LA STOLZ
Yes. Yes. Yes.

VERDI I

Old Barezzi has a huge estate, we'll have our
own house, every evening will bring a feast
and we'll watch sunsets more enchanting
than anywhere else in the world. You've never
been to le Roncole. You think you've seen the
world because you've been to Vienna and
Paris and people have told you about
London. But you've never seen Busseto. With
its towers rising above the cypress trees, and
its hillsides, where we'll go at night and let
ourselves roll down the stairs, all the way to
the fountains.

LA STOLZ

Verdi!

VERDI I

Yes. I am Verdi. He is the one you love. My
own enemy.

LA STOLZ

Enough of this game. Venice is in the past.
Today, I love one man, no matter what his
name is. And that man is you. Tall or short,
dark or fair, stout or lean, anxious or serene,
you are the man I love.

VERDI I

We can leave now.

LA STOLZ

What about *Don Carlo*?

VERDI I

Why this indecision?

LA STOLZ

Giuseppe Verdi, are you going to ask me till
my dying day why I am undecided? Perhaps
it's between me and myself. What if I were to
ask you till the end: "Is it really him? Is it
really you?" Would you tolerate that? I
wouldn't. But today I'm tolerating it. I love
you.

VERDI I

Minister Penco is going to arrive any minute.

LA STOLZ

Don't tell me you're going to flee like a
frightened hare.

VERDI I

Enough of this work. This revolver. This
prison. These shadows, this music. This opera
is sinister. The last act of *Don Carlo* terrifies
me. I loathe tombs.

LA STOLZ

You can leave. I am staying.

VERDI I

I'll force you to come with me.

LA STOLZ

You want force? The entire population of
Milan isn't enough to keep you here? Love

isn't enough? Maestro Verdi, you have to finish *Don Carlo*.

* * * *

We can hear LA STOLZ singing in the wings.

LA STOLZ
  (*off*)
  Tu che le vanità
  Conoscesti del mondo …

VERDI II
  Teresa!

LA STOLZ
  (*sticking her head through the curtain*) Maestro?

VERDI II
  Are you really la Stolz?

LA STOLZ
  (*flabbergasted*) Why?

VERDI II
  If it's really la Stolz, it will be *più forte*.

LA STOLZ
  (*più forte*) *Tu che le vanità conoscesti del mondo …*

VERDI II
    Teresa!

LA STOLZ
    Maestro?

VERDI II
    I love you.

LA STOLZ
    I love you too. Haven't you finished writing
    yet?

VERDI II
    My opera is finished.

LA STOLZ
    Let me see it.

    VERDI II passes her the manuscript. She sings:

LA STOLZ
    Carlo qui verrà …

    *She staggers. For an instant, she thought she
    saw two VERDIs.*

LA STOLZ
    (*breathlessly*) "Are you really Giuseppe Verdi?"

VERDI II
    "Are you really la Stolz?"

LA STOLZ
    Perhaps it is la Benza imitating la Stolz?

VERDI II

And the gondolier pretending to be Verdi?

LA STOLZ

Every garland carved in the ivory of the palazzos of Venice was framed by antique streetlights, and I was left to my own devices. Stolz, who was my husband, was accompanying me, but when I saw you, it seemed to me that only one man among hundreds of look-alikes could be the true Giuseppe Verdi. I left Stolz and walked over to Verdi. I am in love with Verdi. I chose Verdi. I used to love Stolz. But I didn't choose him. Other men before him had come to me. My teachers chose me. *La voce d'oro.* One after the other. *Il colibrì d'amore.* Later, Donizetti chose me. I sang *La Favorita.* But I didn't like that role. I never had a choice, they were the ones—Stolz, who had so little power, Mercadante, who had so little money, Guelfe, who had so little prestige, Donizetti, who had one foot in his grave—they were the ones who chose me. Today, I love one man, the one I chose among a thousand, and that man is you.

> *VERDI II goes over to LA STOLZ and kisses her. VERDI I approaches the couple. LA STOLZ opens her eyes. Studies both men's faces. She is overcome with distress. Moving like a sleepwalker, she goes to the piano, picks up the score and reads:*

"Elisabeth enters and goes to kneel in front of the tomb of Charles V. She senses the end of his reign, the end of the empire, the end of heaven and earth, the disappearance of the universe and the impossibility of any new beginning." You have imagined such immense destruction. Why, Maestro? "She considers her fate as she contemplates the parched earth shrinking beneath the sun's rays. She has renounced all happiness. She renounces all appearances. She fears she will die without having known the truth. She has been betrayed. Tricked." That's how your opera ends? With divine music, but infernal words? Who is this ghost that appears at the very end? He leads Elisabeth and Don Carlo to their death. I am frightened, Maestro, I believed that love would triumph to celebrate Minister Penco's new morning. Instead I enter the music of a terrifying opera to celebrate a funereal wedding? With a king who lies dead in his tomb. (*distressed*) The total work of art. (*She studies VERDI II's face again.*) Where is the man I knew in Venice? The carefree man who tumbled in the sheets with me, who made me happy, and thanks to whom I freed myself from Stolz? I wrote to you at least twelve times. And you replied with letters from the musician. (*crying, she turns to VERDI I*) Why didn't you answer me? Why did you never refer to those moments spent together? Why did you brag about our "little romp" to Mercadante, to la Benza who is so jealous and thrives on other people's unhappiness? (*caressing him*) I chose you among a thousand men, I know it, my arms, my lips, my soul knows it. It was you. You have joined forces to betray me more cruelly, the music, the inspiration, your resemblance, all that is enough to drive me mad, but my body will not betray me. I love you. (*to VERDI II*) I don't know who you are. That's not true, I do know. The man who came to me was named Verdi, like all the others. Why call him by another name? If he is the man I love? (*to VERDI I*) Why did you say: "It's me, Teresa Stolz"? That medal from the Legion of Honour, that bronze cross, do you really think that's where my soul is? (*She removes his medal.*) These gold braids and insignia, and this little V embroidered in scarlet and gold, did you think I was burning with the desire to sleep with your initials? (*She removes his jacket.*) With this collar, these suspenders and these buttons? (*She removes his shirt.*) Did you think I fell in love with fame first? This handsome face, this masculine forehead, might I have loved it only for the seed of opera contained inside? And this head, the hair I caressed in the gondola, why do you think I love it? (*She turns and stares at VERDI II.*) Give me that score. I want to prepare myself for your cadences. Where are the sharps and the flats? Where is the sound of the clarinets? These are tiny rasping sounds that grate on my ear. You must replace them with the flute or the oboe. Or you can simply erase them. Hurry, Maestro, time is of the essence and I think Minister Penco has just arrived. (*turning to speak to both Verdis at once, in an almost frivolous tone*) Please excuse the state I'm in. The total opera is about to begin and I am waiting for a stagefright that refuses to come. This lack of stagefright is upsetting. I must tend to my makeup.

> *LA STOLZ picks up the revolver and disappears behind the curtain.*

* * * *

> *VERDI II puts on THE PROMPTER's clothes again.*

THE PROMPTER
(*to VERDI*) Well, what are you waiting for? The crowd outside is restless. You must meet the Opposition. Go on, hurry, they're getting impatient. Perhaps they've already managed to break down the doors. Faster! They'll do anything. A betrayed people is a violent people. Faster! Outside the doors, they're

chanting the name Verdi. *In testa che avete, signor Ceprano? Ei sbuffa! Vedete?* Italy in all its splendour, in the eyes of the last of the buffoons contemplating the last of the kings. And you are the one they have chosen.

>*Gunshot from behind the curtain. VERDI rushes onto the stage.*

* * * *

>*THE DIRECTOR and TERZIANI are waiting for the curtain to rise.*

TERZIANI
(*worried*) The strangest thing. I'm telling you, it's incomprehensible.

THE DIRECTOR
What's the matter, Terziani?

TERZIANI
Minister Penco is very undecided. He doesn't dare venture into the crowd. He suspects a plot. Apparently he received a letter this morning from the maestro stating he never agreed to compose an opera for the new Party.

In a foul mood, THE DIRECTOR shrugs his shoulders and stares at the curtain.

THE DIRECTOR
What are we waiting for? Isn't this curtain ever going to rise?

Second gunshot from behind the curtain.

THE DIRECTOR
My God! What's that? It's me they're after! What is going on?!

He stands up and heads for the stage.

THE PROMPTER
(*appearing through the trapdoor*) Stay where you are.

THE DIRECTOR
But that gunshot ... Is there no end to the gunshots? Such powerful, deadly noises—like the metronome of death. What are they doing behind the curtain?

He sits down again. The curtain rises. On stage, LA STOLZ and VERDI are lying in a pool of blood.

THE DIRECTOR
Ooooh! How prodigious! What an inspired beginning! Verdi himself, in his own opera. He was right, who needs an overture, just look at the opening tableau. I love the idea that the total opera begins with a dream. But

what was that gunshot? Oh, Verdi … Verdi?
(*He walks to the edge of the stage, imploring
Terziani and the prompter, going from one to the
other.*) Verdi … ? Verdi … ?

THE PROMPTER
Verdi? … Why, signor Mariani, didn't Minister
Penco advise you? Verdi is in Cairo!

End.